Lodore Falls

FA
LA
RECIPES

compiled by

Carole Gregory

with illustrations

by A.R.Quinton

SALMON

INDEX

Cover pictures: *front* The Langdale Pikes *back* Ullswater and Helvellyn

Printed and Published by J. Salmon Ltd., Sevenoaks, England ©

Lakeland Lemon Cake

8 oz. self-raising flour
6 oz. butter
6 oz. caster sugar
Pinch of salt
Pinch of ground cinnamon
½ level teaspoon ground ginger
2 large eggs, beaten
Grated rind, and juice of 1 large lemon
1 tablespoon milk

Set oven to 325°F or Mark 3. Grease and line the base and sides of a 7 inch round cake tin. In a bowl cream the butter and sugar until pale and fluffy. Add the beaten eggs, salt, cinnamon, ginger, sieve in the flour and mix well. Add the lemon rind and juice and then add the milk. Mix well and place in the prepared tin. Level the top and bake for about 1 hour until firm and pale brown. Leave in the tin for 15 minutes and then transfer to a wire rack. Keep for 48 hours before cutting. Either serve plain or cut in half and sandwich with homemade lemon curd.

Ullswater and Helvellyn

Westmorland Parkin

1 lb. porridge oats
8 oz. flour
1 lb. black treacle
8 oz. butter
8 oz. demerara sugar
1 teaspoon allspice
1 teaspoon salt
2 teaspoons baking powder
2 teaspoons ground ginger
3 oz. milk
1 teaspoon bicarbonate of soda
1 small egg, beaten

Set oven to 350°F or Mark 4. Well grease and line a deep roasting tin 10 inches x 13 inches. Place all the dry ingredients into a large mixing bowl. Gently heat the treacle and butter together in a saucepan until melted and pour into the dry mixture. Stir well, add the beaten egg and stir again. Warm the milk, add it to mixture and beat well. Pour into the tin and bake for 1–1½ hours until firm. Leave in the tin for ½ hour then turn out on to a wire rack. Keep for 48 hours then cut into squares.

Ennerdale Cake

1 rounded teaspoon baking powder
10 oz. flour
6 oz. caster sugar
6 oz. butter
6 oz. lard
1 large egg, beaten
Pinch of salt
Raspberry jam

Set oven to 325°F or Mark 3. Grease and flour a shallow 7 inch square tin. Sieve the flour, baking powder and salt into a mixing bowl. Take the butter and lard direct from the refridgerator, cut into small pieces and, with the fingertips, mix lightly into the flour to a stiff, crumbly paste. Add the sugar and the beaten egg and mix well. Turn out the mixture on to a very well-floured board and divide in half. Lightly flatten and mould one half, put into the tin and press out evenly to the corners. Spread with a layer of raspberry jam. Flatten and mould the other half of the mixture, place on top of the jam and press out evenly to the corners. Press round edges with a fork. Bake for about 40–60 minutes until light golden brown. Leave in the tin to cool but cut into small squares while warm. Dredge the top with a little sieved icing sugar.

Lakeland Tatie Scones

8 oz. self-raising flour
4 oz. boiled mashed potatoes
2 oz. strong cheese, grated
1 oz. lard
Pinch of salt
Pinch of freshly grated nutmeg
Freshly ground black pepper
A little milk

Set oven to 400°F or Mark 6. Sieve the flour into a mixing bowl. Add the lard and rub in with the fingertips. Add the rest of the ingredients and mix well. Add enough milk to make a stiff dough. Roll out on a floured board to ½ inch thickness. Cut into 3 inch rounds and either place on greased baking sheets in the oven and brown for 10 minutes on either side, or fry in hot fat for a few minutes each side until golden brown. Serve hot with butter. It is also nice served with rashers of home cured bacon.

Windermere Spice Biscuits

4 oz. butter or hard margarine
4 oz. sugar
1 teaspoon caraway seeds
6 oz. flour
½ teaspoon ground cinnamon
Pinch of salt
1 large egg, beaten

Set oven to 350°F or Mark 4. Beat the butter and sugar together in a bowl until fluffy. Add the beaten egg, then the salt, cinnamon and caraway seeds and sieve in the flour. Roll out to ¼ inch thickness and cut with a biscuit cutter. Place on greased baking sheets and bake for about 20 minutes. Cool on a wire rack. Should make about 20 biscuits.

Belle Isle and Bowness, Windermere

Butter Bean Hotpot

One 15 oz. tin tomatoes
1 lb. butter beans
(soaked overnight)
1 tablespoon black treacle
1 pint boiling water
8 oz. bacon pieces, de-rinded
1 oz. demerara sugar
1 level teaspoon dry mustard powder
Bay leaf and pinch of mixed herbs
Freshly ground nutmeg to taste
Freshly ground black pepper to taste

Set oven to 300°F or Mark 2. Drain the beans and place in a deep, buttered casserole dish. Add the bacon pieces. In a bowl mix the sugar, mustard powder and treacle with the boiling water. Add the tomatoes to the treacle mixture, stir well and pour over the beans and bacon. Add the bay leaf, nutmeg, herbs and black pepper. Stir well. Cover with a tight fitting lid and bake for 3 hours. Add more water after 2 hours if the hotpot is too thick. Serve with baked potatoes, which can be baked in the oven at the same time. Add salt if needed just before serving. Serves 4.

Cartmel Cream Cake

CAKE
6 oz. soft margarine
6 oz. caster sugar
6 oz. self-raising flour
Pinch of salt
3 large eggs, beaten

SYRUP
3 oz. granulated sugar
6 oz. water
2 tablespoons rum
2 tablespoons coffee essence

DECORATION
½ pint whipped double cream
A ring of cherries and hazelnuts
Grated chocolate in the centre

Set oven to 350°F or Mark 4. Grease and line the base and sides of a deep 8 inch round cake tin. In a bowl cream the margarine and sugar well. Add the beaten eggs, and salt, sieve in the flour and mix well. Place in the tin, level the top and bake for about 40 minutes until firm. Leave in the tin for 15 minutes then turn out on to a large, deep dish. Meanwhile heat the sugar and water together in a saucepan and stir until the sugar has dissolved. Remove from the heat, add the rum and coffee essence and stir well. Prick the top of the cake all over with a skewer and pour the *warm* syrup over the *warm* cake. Leave the cake for at least 4 hours to absorb the liquid then coat over all with cream and decorate with cherries and nuts and grated chocolate. Serve chilled. Serves 8–10.

Friar's Crag, Derwentwater

Cumberland Nickies

8 oz. shortcrust pastry
3 oz. currants
1 tablespoon demerara sugar
Good pinch of grated nutmeg
1 oz. butter
1 tablespoon rum

Set oven to 400°F or Mark 6. Melt the butter in a saucepan, add the currants, sugar, nutmeg and rum and mix well. Leave to cool. Roll out the pastry thinly, cut into 3 inch rounds and brush edges with water. Place a little fruit mixture in centre of one round and top it with another round; seal the edges well. Prick top with a fork and place on a baking sheet. Bake for 10–15 minutes then cool on a wire rack. Makes about 8–10.

Elderberry Pie

1 lb. elderberries, cleaned and dried
1 level tablespoon cornflour
Juices of ½ lemon
Sugar to taste; about 3 oz.
6 oz. shortcrust pastry
Small egg, beaten

Set oven to 375°F or Mark 5. Roll out the pastry and use half to line a shallow 8 inch pie plate. Mix the fruit, sugar, cornflour and lemon juice together and place on the pastry. Brush the edges with beaten egg and cover with the rest of the pastry. Seal the edges and brush the top with beaten egg. Bake for 20–30 minutes until golden. Sprinkle the top with caster sugar and serve, just warm, with whipped cream. Alternatively leave until completely cold and spread a very thin layer of lemon glacé icing on top. Serve the same day for tea.

Lonsdale Scones

12 oz. flour
1 rounded tablespoon sugar
1 level teaspoon bicarbonate of soda
3½ oz. lard
2 level teaspoons cream of tartar
Enough milk to make a soft dough

Set oven to 400°F or Mark 6. Sieve the flour, cream of tartar and bicarbonate of soda into a bowl. Rub in the lard with the fingertips. Mix in the sugar. Make a soft dough with the milk. Roll out on a floured board to ¾ inch thickness. Cut into rounds with a 2½ inch plain biscuit cutter. Brush the tops lightly with milk and bake on greased baking sheets for about 15 minutes. Store in an airtight tin and serve buttered. Makes about 14 scones.

Honister Toffee

8 oz. granulated sugar
3 oz. butter (NOT margarine)
2 tablespoons golden syrup
1 small tin evaporated milk

Well butter a 9 inch x 7 inch shallow tin. Place butter, sugar and syrup into a large heavy saucepan and heat gently, stirring constantly, until the sugar has dissolved. Add the milk and boil steadily until the mixture is much darker and thicker, stirring all the time. This takes about 20 minutes. Immediately pour into prepared tin and break into pieces when set. Store in an airtight tin.

Honister Pass

Turnip Pie

1½ lb. turnips (or swede or parsnips), peeled
8 oz. milk
2 tablespoons cream
Freshly grated nutmeg
Pinch of mixed herbs
4 oz. Cheddar cheese, grated
5 oz. fresh breadcrumbs
Salt and black pepper
2 oz. butter

Set oven to 375°F or Mark 5. Butter a casserole dish. Peel the turnips and cut in quarters and then slice thinly. Boil in salted water until almost tender. Drain well and arrange in the casserole. Season well and sprinkle with herbs and nutmeg. Pour on the milk and cream. Mix the cheese and breadcrumbs together and sprinkle over the turnips. Dot with butter and bake, uncovered, for 30–40 minutes until well browned. Serve with cold bacon or roasts. The small white turnips are very tasty served like this. Serves 4–5.

Buttermere Biscuits

8 oz. flour
4 oz. butter
4 oz. caster sugar
Grated rind of 1 lemon
½ level teaspoon baking powder
1 large egg, beaten
Pinch of salt
Pinch of ground cinnamon
1½ oz. currants, washed and dried

Set oven to 350°F or Mark 4. Sieve the flour and salt into a mixing bowl. Rub the butter into the flour until it resembles fine breadcrumbs. Add the sugar, currants, lemon rind, baking powder and cinnamon. Bind with the beaten egg and knead the mixture lightly. Roll out to ¼ inch thickness on a lightly floured surface, and cut with a fluted biscuit cutter. Place on greased baking trays and bake for 15–20 minutes until pale brown. Cool on a wire rack. Makes about 30 biscuits.

Grasmere from Red Bank

Grasmere Gingerbread

8 oz. butter or hard margarine
8 oz. soft brown sugar
1 lb. flour
2 level teaspoons ground ginger
1 level teaspoon cream of tartar
1 level teaspoon bicarbonate of soda
Pinch of salt
1 tablespoon golden syrup

Set oven to 325°F or Mark 3. Grease a shallow, oblong tin 12 inches x 7 inches. Beat together the butter and sugar in a mixing bowl. Stir in the syrup then add the rest of the ingredients, sieved together, and mix well. Put the mixture into the tin and press down firmly with a floured fork. Bake for 40–60 minutes. Leave in the tin until cold but cut into fingers while still warm. Store in an airtight tin.

Blackberry and Apple Pudding

1 lb. cooking apples, peeled, cored and thinly sliced
1 pint water
1 lb. blackberries, washed
6 oz. sugar
8–12 slices white bread, crusts removed

Simmer the fruit in the water until just tender. Stir in the sugar until dissolved. Cool. Cut a circle of bread to fit the base of a 2 lb. pudding basin, cut wedge shaped slices of bread and line the sides of the basin. Fill one third of the basin with the fruit mixture, cover with a circle of bread then add more fruit and another circle of bread. Fill the basin until almost full then add a final circle of bread. Cover with a plate which fits the top of the basin and place a weight on top. Leave in the refrigerator for 24–48 hours. Turn out carefully. Serve with whipped cream. Serves 8. Any left-over fruit mixture can be strained and the juice poured over the pudding when ready to be served.

Lardy Johns

8 oz. flour
Pinch of salt
3 oz. lard
2 oz. sugar
2 oz. currants
Cold water to mix

Set oven to 400°F or Mark 6. Sieve the flour and salt into a mixing bowl. Rub in the lard until the mixture is crumbly. Stir in the sugar and the currants and mix to a stiff dough with the water. Roll out on a floured surface to ¼ inch thickness and cut into 2 inch squares. Place on a greased baking tray and bake for about 15 minutes. Makes about 12 Lardy Johns. Best eaten the same day – served just warm, split with a knob of butter in the centre.

Nutty Dainties

4 oz. hard margarine
4 oz. rolled oats
1½ tablespoons golden syrup
4 oz. sugar
4 oz. dessicated coconut

Set oven to 325°F or Mark 3. Well grease a Swiss Roll tin. Place the oats, sugar and coconut in a mixing bowl and stir to mix. Gently melt the syrup and margarine together in a saucepan, pour into the bowl and mix well. Place in the tin and press down with a floured fork. Bake for about 20 minutes until golden brown. Leave in the tin to cool, but cut into fingers while still warm.

The Head of Derwentwater

Leek and Bacon Savoury

1 lb. leeks, washed and thinly sliced
8 oz. bacon pieces, de-rinded
1½ lb. cold, cooked sliced potatoes
Pinch of mixed herbs
Pinch of nutmeg
1 pint well seasoned cheese sauce
3 oz. Cheddar cheese, grated
2 oz. butter
Freshly ground black pepper

Set oven to 350°F or Mark 4. Melt the butter in frying pan and cook the leeks for 5 minutes, stirring often. Remove from the heat. Grease a shallow casserole dish. Place half the potato slices in the base of the dish and then add the leeks. Season well. Add the bacon and top with the remainder of the potatoes. Season again with nutmeg and herbs. Cover with the cheese sauce. Sprinkle the grated cheese on top. Bake, uncovered, for 30–40 minutes. Serve at once. Serves 4.

Honey Fruit Biscuits

8 oz. self-raising flour
1 level teaspoon clear honey
4 oz. butter
4 oz. soft brown sugar
1 large egg
1 oz. chocolate chips
Grated rind of 1 orange
2 oz. finely chopped nuts
Pinch of salt

Set oven to 350°F or Mark 4. Cream the butter and sugar together in a mixing bowl until soft. Beat in the egg and honey and stir in the nuts, grated rind, chocolate chips and salt. Sieve in the flour and mix well. Divide the mixture into balls each the size of a walnut. Place about 2 inches apart on greased baking trays and flatten slightly with a floured fork. Bake for 10–15 minutes until pale brown. Leave to cool for a few minutes and then transfer to a wire rack. Makes about 36 biscuits.

Grange-in-Borrowdale

Borrowdale Teabread

9 oz. flour
9 oz. strong hot tea
½ level teaspoon bicarbonate of soda
1 large egg, beaten
1 lb. mixed dried fruit
6 oz. soft brown sugar
Grated rind of 1 orange and 1 lemon
1 oz. melted butter
Pinch of freshly grated nutmeg

Place the fruit in a mixing bowl. Add the sugar, and then pour on the hot tea. Stir well, cover and leave overnight. Next day; set oven to 325°F or Mark 3. Well grease a 2 lb. loaf tin. To the fruit mixture add the beaten egg, the melted butter, the grated rind, and the nutmeg and mix well. Sieve the flour and bicarbonate of soda together on to the mixture and fold in until well blended. Pour into the prepared tin and bake for about 1 hour until firm. Leave in the tin for 30 minutes then turn out on to a wire rack. When cold, keep in a tin for 24 hours to improve the flavour. Serve sliced and buttered.

Honister Cheesecake

8 oz. rich shortcrust pastry
8 oz. cream cheese
4 oz. caster sugar
Juices and rind of 1 lemon
5 oz. whipped double cream
5 oz. natural yoghurt
1 packet gelatine (½ oz.) sprinkled over 1 fl. oz. of hot water, stirred until dissolved
Grated chocolate and mandarin slices for decoration

Set oven to 375°F or Mark 5. Line an 8 inch flan ring with the shortcrust pastry and bake "blind" for 20 minutes. Allow to cool before filling. Alternatively use a biscuit crust made of 4 oz. crushed digestive biscuits, 2 oz. melted butter and 1 oz. caster sugar, mixed together and pressed into a flan ring lined with foil. Cook as above and allow to cool.

Filling – Mix the cheese, sugar, rind and juice of the lemon together until smooth. Add the yoghurt and the whipped cream. Lastly add the dissolved gelatine and stir the mixture gently for a few minutes. Pour into the flan case and leave to set. Decorate with grated chocolate and mandarin slices. Chill before serving. This is a rich cheesecake and may be served plain or with single cream if preferred. Serves 8.

Egremont Cake

9 oz. self-raising flour
1 oz. cocoa powder
7 oz. caster sugar
1 large egg, beaten
1 oz. golden syrup
4 oz. hard margarine
6 oz. tepid milk
½ level teaspoon bicarbonate of soda mixed with 3 oz. hot water
Pinch of salt

Set oven to 350°F or Mark 4. Grease and line a 7 inch square deep cake tin. Sieve the flour, cocoa and salt into a mixing bowl. Add the sugar. Warm the syrup and margarine until melted, add to flour and mix well. Add the beaten egg and tepid milk and mix well. Then add bicarbonate of soda mixture and blend in. Pour into the prepared tin. Bake for 30–40 minutes until firm. Leave in the tin for 15 minutes, then turn out on to a wire rack. When cold cut across the middle and sandwich with chocolate butter icing. Dredge the top with a little sieved icing sugar.

Cumberland Apple Pudding

1½ lb. cooking apples, stewed, and sweetened to taste
8 oz. self-raising flour
4 oz. hard margarine
4 oz. soft brown sugar
1 level teaspoon ground ginger
Pinch of salt

Set oven to 375°F or Mark 5. Butter a pie dish and put the stewed apples in the bottom. Sieve the flour, salt and ginger into a mixing bowl. Rub in the margarine and stir in the sugar. Spread this mixture over the apples and bake for 30 minutes. Serve with cream or custard. Serves 4–5.

Derwentwater and Skiddaw

Boiled Bacon

3½–4 lb. bacon joint
(soaked overnight)
6 cloves
6 peppercorns
2 inch stick of cinnamon
Piece of lemon rind without pith
3 teaspoons black treacle
½ pint pineapple juice or dry cider

FOR GLAZE
3 tablespoons demerara sugar
1 teaspoon ground cinnamon
3 teaspoons dry mustard powder

Place the joint in a large pan and cover with fresh cold water. Bring to the boil and remove any scum. Add the cloves, peppercorns, cinnamon stick, lemon rind and treacle. Simmer gently for 1½ hours, adding more boiling water if necessary. Remove from the heat, take the bacon out and remove the rind. Set oven to 425°F or Mark 7. Mix all the glaze ingredients together and press this mixture firmly on to the bacon fat. Place the bacon in a roasting tin with the glazed side uppermost. Add the pineapple juice or cider and bake, uncovered, for 30 minutes until golden brown. Serve hot or cold with mustard sauce. Serves 8.

Currant Pasties

4 oz. currants
2 oz. soft brown sugar
½ level teaspoon ground cinnamon
Pinch of grated nutmeg
1 dessertspoon rum
1 small cooking apple, peeled, cored and finely diced
2½ oz. butter
1½ oz. lard
6 oz. flour
Pinch of salt
Beaten egg to seal pastry

Set oven to 400°F or Mark 6. Grease baking trays. Place the currants, sugar, cinnamon, nutmeg, apple and rum in a bowl. Mix well. Add 1 oz. of the butter cut up into small pieces and stir the mixture. Into another bowl, sieve the flour and salt. Rub in the remainder of the butter and the lard until the mixture resembles breadcrumbs. Add enough cold water to make a stiff dough. Roll out on a floured surface and cut into 12 circles using a 4 inch plain cutter. Place a small spoonful of the fruit mixture on each circle and brush egg round edges. Fold each circle in half and seal the edges well with a fork. Brush with egg and bake for 20 minutes until golden brown. Sprinkle with caster sugar. Makes 12 pasties.

Windermere from Low Wood

AMBLESIDE GINGERBREAD

1 lb. flour
2 level teaspoons baking powder
1 oz. ground ginger
4 oz. lard
5 oz. demerara sugar
3 oz. chopped crystallised ginger
8 oz. golden syrup
1 beaten egg
Pinch of salt
Pinch of nutmeg
¼ pint milk

Set oven to 350°F or Mark 4. Grease and line an 11 inch x 7 inch deep tin. Sieve the flour, salt, baking powder and ground ginger into a large bowl. Cut the lard into small pieces and rub in with the fingertips. Stir in the sugar, crystallised ginger and nutmeg. Warm the syrup and milk together in a pan then pour on to the dry ingredients and mix well. Add the beaten egg and mix again. Pour into the prepared tin and bake for 1–1¼ hours until firm. Leave in the tin for ½ hour, then turn out on to a wire rack. Cut into squares. This gingerbread keeps well.

Savoury Pudding

6 oz. finely chopped suet
4 oz. self-raising flour
1 heaped teaspoon dried sage
1 heaped teaspoon dried marjoram
Salt and black pepper
½ teaspoon baking powder
4 oz. fresh breadcrumbs
1 dessertspoon finely chopped onion
2 eggs
Milk to mix, about ½–¾ pint

Set oven to 425°F or Mark 7. Place all the ingredients except the eggs and milk into a large mixing bowl. Beat in the eggs and add sufficient milk to form a batter. Pour into a hot roasting tin, which has a thin layer of hot fat in the bottom. Bake for about 20–30 minutes. Eat with a pork roast. It can be cooked at the same time. Serves 4–6.

Wholemeal Scones

½ lb. wholemeal flour
½ lb. self-raising flour
½ level teaspoon salt
½ level teaspoon cream of tartar
½ level teaspoon bicarbonate of soda
Pinch of nutmeg
4 oz. hard margarine
1 dessertspoon sugar
4 oz. chopped dates or sultanas
About ½ pint milk or buttermilk

Set oven to 375°F or Mark 5. Put the flour, salt, cream of tartar, bicarbonate of soda and nutmeg into a mixing bowl and mix well. Rub in the margarine with the fingertips. Stir in the sugar and the dates or sultanas. Add sufficient milk to make a soft dough. Roll out to ¾ inch thickness on a floured surface and cut into triangles. Place on greased baking trays and brush the tops with milk. Bake for 15–20 minutes until golden. Delicious eaten the same day with butter and damson jam. Makes about 18 triangles.

Cumberland Sauce

Grated rind and juice of
1 lemon and 1 orange
2 oz. water
Salt and black pepper
2 tablespoons vinegar
4 level tablespoons redcurrant jelly
1 level tablespoon made mustard
2 tablespoons port, or elderberry wine

Grate the lemon and orange rinds and place them in a small saucepan with the water and boil for 5 minutes. Add the rest of the ingredients and stir until the jelly has melted. Check the seasoning. Serve with ham, lamb or game.

Grisedale and Helvellyn

Rum Butter

8 oz. unsalted butter
1 lb. soft brown sugar
1 wineglass of rum
Freshly grated nutmeg to taste

Soften the butter slightly and beat it well. Beat in the sugar and nutmeg and gradually beat in the rum. Place in a pretty dish, level the top and leave to set. Serve with scones, mince pies, Christmas pudding or on hot freshly made toast at teatime. Often served at Christening Parties.

Kendal Mint Cake

1 lb. granulated sugar
¼ pint milk
1 teaspoon peppermint essence
6 oz. plain chocolate, melted (optional)

A sugar thermometer

Well butter a 7 inch square shallow tin. Place the sugar and milk in a large heavy-based saucepan. Heat gently until the sugar has dissolved, then bring to the boil and boil steadily until the sugar thermometer reads 240°F. Remove the pan from the heat. Add the essence and beat the mixture well until it is smooth. Pour into the prepared tin and, as it sets, mark into squares with a knife. For brown mint cake use 1 lb. soft brown sugar instead of the granulated sugar. For a special treat, cover with melted plain chocolate and leave to set.

The Head of Ullswater

Cumberland Sand Cake

2 oz. butter
4 oz. caster sugar
1 oz. flour
4 oz. cornflour
1 level teaspoon baking powder
2 beaten eggs
2 teaspoons fresh lemon juice
Pinch of salt
Pinch of grated nutmeg

Set oven to 350°F or Mark 4. Grease and line a 2 inch deep, 7 inch round cake tin. Cream the butter and sugar well together in a mixing bowl, add the eggs and beat well. Fold in the sieved flour, the salt and nutmeg. Lastly add the lemon juice and mix well. Place in the tin and level the top. Bake for about 30 minutes until firm and golden. Leave in the tin for 15 minutes then turn out on to a wire rack. Dredge the top with a little sieved icing sugar.

Apple Delight

1 lb. cooking apples, peeled and thinly sliced
2 oz. butter
4 oz. caster sugar
2 oz. raisins or sultanas
5 oz. white wine or cider
Pinch of freshly grated nutmeg
½ level teaspoon ground cinnamon
2 oz. self-raising flour
Pinch of salt
2 medium eggs
2 oz. thick cream

Set oven to 350°F or Mark 4. Grease an 8 inch pie dish. Melt the butter gently in a saucepan and add the wine or cider and half the sugar; stir until dissolved. Add the spices, raisins or sultanas and the apple slices. Poach gently until the fruit is almost tender. Place this fruit mixture carefully into the pie dish. Then sieve the flour and salt into a mixing bowl. Add remaining sugar and the eggs and beat well. Fold in the cream until well blended and pour on top of the apple mixture. Bake for about 30 minutes until brown and firm. Dust with caster sugar. Serve warm with a jug of cream. Serves 4.

Carrot Cake

8 oz. soft brown sugar
2 oz. water
8 oz. carrot, peeled and grated
4 oz. raisins or currants
1 lb. flour
3 oz. butter
1 level teaspoon salt
1 level teaspoon bicarbonate of soda
2 level teaspoons baking powder
½ level teaspoon mixed spice
2 level teaspoons ground cinnamon
4 oz. chopped nuts
1 beaten egg

Set oven to 325°F or Mark 3. Well grease a deep 7 inch square tin. Place the water, sugar, raisins or currants, carrot, spices and butter into a saucepan and set on a low heat until the sugar has dissolved, stirring all the time. Then boil for 3 minutes. Remove from the heat and leave until the mixture is tepid, then stir in the sieved flour, salt, baking powder, bicarbonate of soda, nuts and the beaten egg. Mix well together. Place in the tin and bake for about 1 hour until firm. Leave in the tin for 15 minutes and then turn out on to a wire rack. Keep for 24 hours before serving. Serve sliced and buttered. This cake keeps well.

METRIC CONVERSIONS

The weights, measures and oven temperatures used in the preceding recipes can be easily converted to their metric equivalents.

Weights

Avoirdupois	Metric
1 oz.	just under 30 grams
4 oz. (¼ lb.)	app. 115 grams
8 oz. (½ lb.)	app. 230 grams
1 lb.	454 grams

Liquid Measures

Imperial	Metric
1 tablespoon (liquid only)	20 millilitres
1 fl. oz.	app. 30 millilitres
1 gill (¼ pt.)	app. 145 millilitres
½ pt.	app. 285 millilitres
1 pt.	app. 570 millilitres
1 qt.	app. 1.140 litres

Oven Temperatures

	°Fahrenheit	Gas Mark	°Celsius
Slow	300	2	140
	325	3	158
Moderate	350	4	177
	375	5	190
	400	6	204
Hot	425	7	214
	450	8	232
	500	9	260

Flour as specified in these recipes refers to Plain Flour unless otherwise described